WITHDRAWN

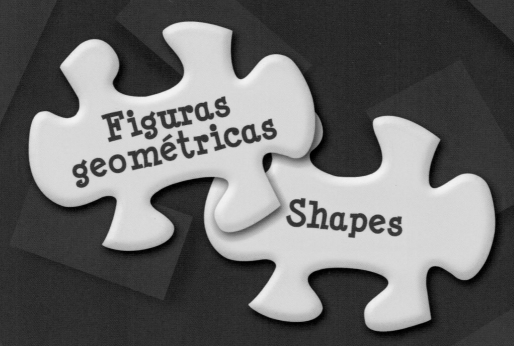

Figuras geométricas

Shapes

Rectángulos/Rectangles

por/by Sarah L. Schuette

Traducción/Translation: Dr. Martín Luis Guzmán Ferrer

Asesora literaria/Reading Consultant:

Dra. Elena Bodrova, asesora principal/Senior Consultant

Mid-continent Research for Education and Learning

A+ books
BILINGÜE/BILINGUAL

CAPSTONE PRESS
a capstone imprint

A+ Books are published by Capstone Press,
1710 Roe Crest Drive, North Mankato, Minnesota 56003.
www.capstonepub.com

092011
006330R

 Books published by Capstone Press are manufactured with
paper containing at least 10 percent post-consumer waste.

Library of Congress Cataloging-in-Publication Data
Schuette, Sarah L., 1976–
    [Rectangles. Spanish & English]
    Réctangulos : réctangulos a nuestro alrededor = Rectangles : seeing rectangles all around us /
por Sarah L. Schuette.
       p. cm. — (A+ bilingüe. Figuras geométricas = A+ bilingual. Shapes)
    Summary: "Simple text, photographs, and illustrations show rectangles in everyday objects — in both
English and Spanish" — Provided by publisher.
    Includes index.
    ISBN 978-1-4296-4586-7 (lib. bdg.)
    1. Rectangles — Juvenile literature. I. Title. II. Series.
QA482.S3818 2010
516'.154 — dc22   2009040926

Created by the A+ Team

Sarah L. Schuette, editor; Katy Kudela bilingual editor; Adalin Torres-Zayas, Spanish copy editor;
    Heather Kindseth, art director and designer; Jason Knudson, designer and illustrator;
    Angi Gahler, illustrator; Gary Sundermeyer, photographer; Nancy White, photo stylist;
    Eric Manske, production specialist

Note to Parents, Teachers, and Librarians
The Figuras geométricas/Shapes series uses color photographs and a nonfiction format to introduce
children to the shapes around them in both English and Spanish. It is designed to be read aloud to
a pre-reader or to be read independently by an early reader. The images help early readers and
listeners understand the text and concepts discussed. The book encourages further learning by
including the following sections: Table of Contents, Glossary, Internet Sites, and Index. Early readers
may need assistance using these features.

Table of Contents/
Tabla de contenidos

4

Rectangles have four sides, two short and two long.

Los rectángulos tienen cuatro lados, dos cortos y dos largos.

3 + 2 = 5

5 - 1 = ?

Todo el mundo comete errores. Por suerte, tú puedes corregir fácilmente errores en tu tarea con un borrador.

Everyone makes mistakes. Luckily, you can easily fix mistakes on your homework with an eraser.

They rub out the answers you write that are wrong.

Con ellos borras las respuestas equivocadas que escribiste.

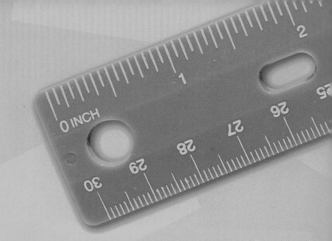

Rectangles can measure and draw straight lines.

- - - - - - - - - - - - - -

Con los rectángulos puedes medir y dibujar líneas rectas.

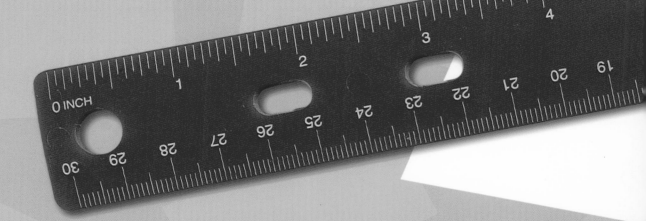

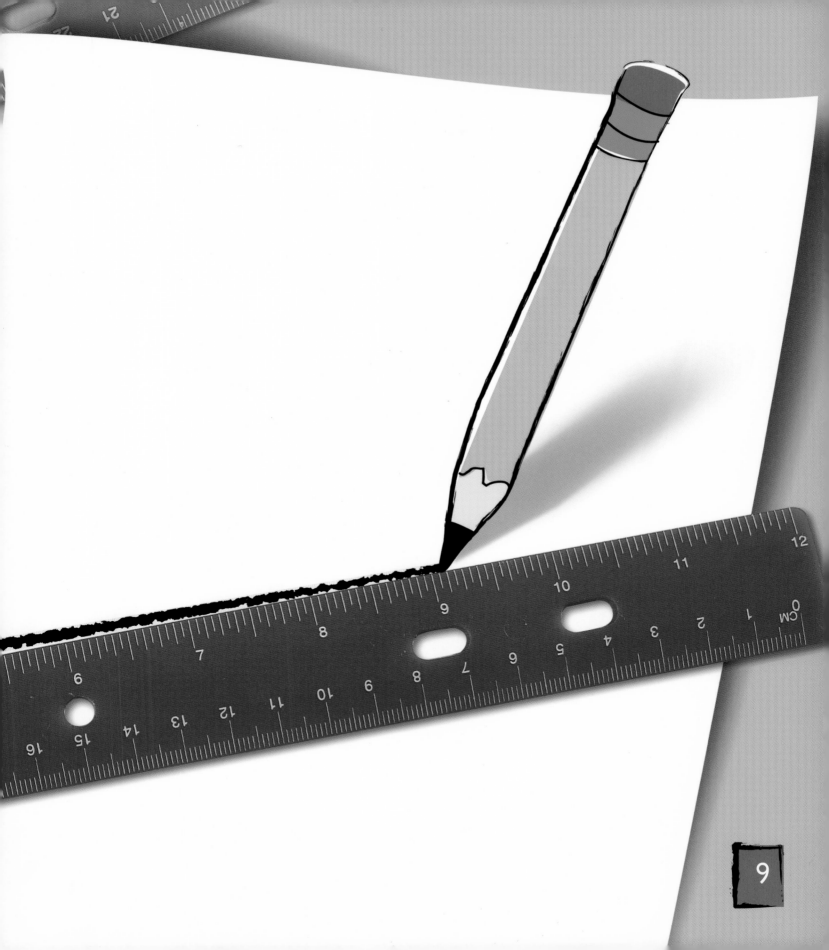

10

Speed limit signs tell drivers about safe speeds. Traffic signs come in many different shapes and colors.

Las señales de límite de velocidad indican a los conductores cuáles velocidades son seguras. Las señales de tránsito vienen en muchas formas y colores diferentes.

Rectangles are white speed limit signs.

Los rectángulos son señales blancas de límite de velocidad.

Fifty-two
rectangles
make up a deck.

- - - - - - - - - - - - - -

Cincuenta y dos
rectángulos hacen
una baraja.

13

14

On your birthday, you might get a check.

En tu cumpleaños es posible que te regalen un cheque.

Banks will give you money when you exchange a check for cash. Then you can save your money or buy a fun treat.

Los bancos te dan dinero cuando cambias un cheque por efectivo. Puedes guardar tu dinero o comprarte un antojo divertido.

15

You use rectangles when you pay.

Tú usas rectángulos cuando haces un pago.

Did you know that most pianos have 88 black and white keys? Musical notes tell players which keys to press on the piano. Some piano players can even play without reading music.

¿Sabías que la mayoría de los pianos tienen 88 teclas blancas o negras? Las notas musicales le dicen al pianista qué teclas debe tocar en el piano. Hay algunos pianistas que hasta pueden tocar sin leer la música.

Piano keys are rectangles you play.

Las teclas del piano son rectángulos que tú puedes tocar.

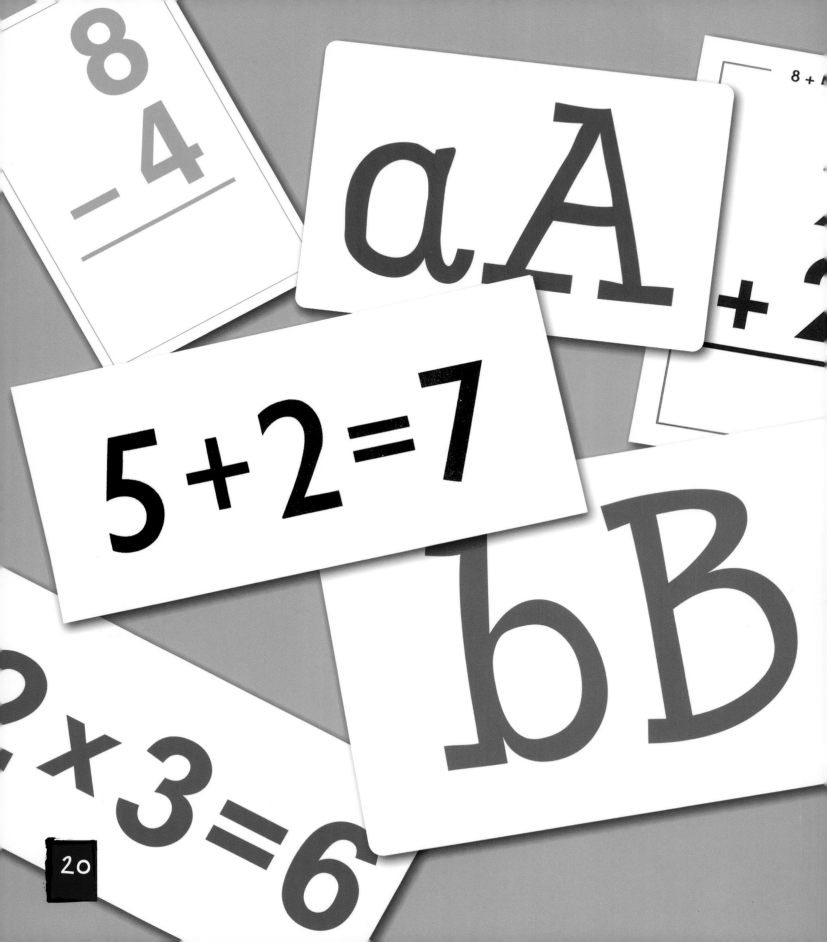

Use flash rectangles
at your school.

- - - - - - - - - - - - - - -

En tu escuela usas
tarjetas rectangulares
para estudiar.

21

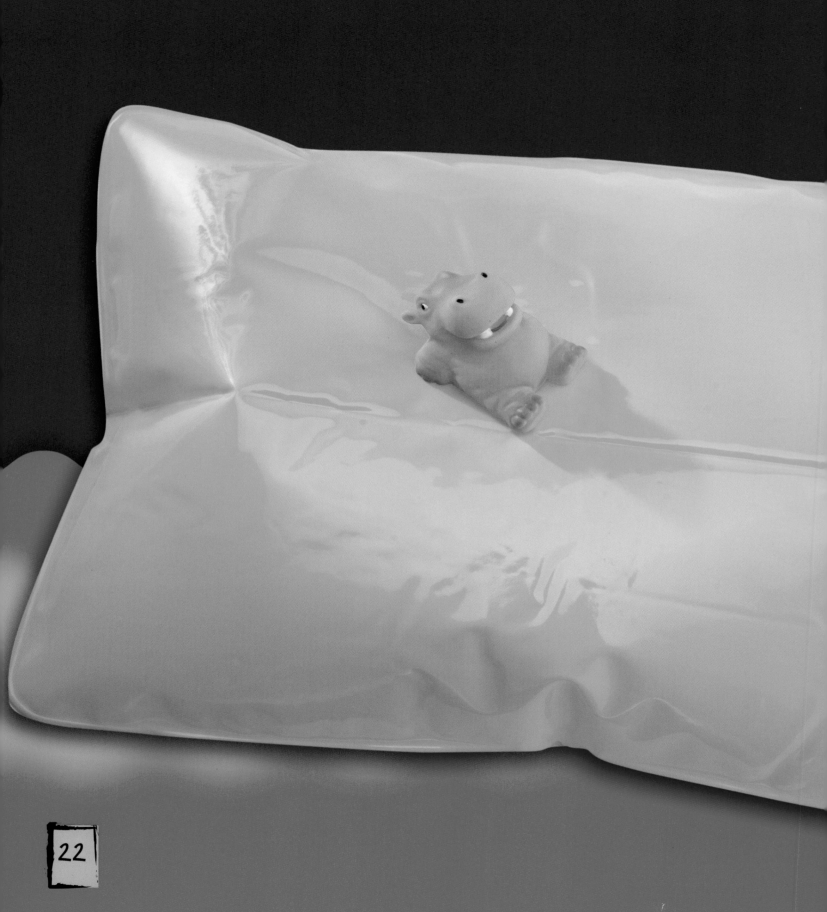

A rectangle can even float in your pool.

Un rectángulo hasta puede flotar en tu alberca.

24

It is fun to chew gum and blow bubbles. If you ever get gum stuck in your hair, use peanut butter to get it out.

Es divertido mascar chicle y hacer globitos. Si se te pega el chicle en el pelo, usa mantequilla de maní o cacahuate para quitártelo.

Sticks of gum are rectangles you chew.

Los chicles son rectángulos que masticas.

Find the rectangle
that sticks on you.

26

Encuentra el rectángulo
que tienes pegado.

Build a Rectangle Town/
Vamos a construir una ciudad de rectángulos

You will need/
Necesitas:

graham crackers/
galletas *graham*

cookie sheet/
una bandeja para galletas

tubes of frosting/
tubos de glaseado

plastic spoon/
una cuchara de plástico

colored sprinkles/
chispitas de colores

gel icing/
glaseado de jalea

1 Break a few of the large crackers into smaller rectangle pieces. Arrange the pieces on the cookie sheet.

SNAP!

1 Parte unas cuantas galletas en rectángulos pequeños. Coloca las piezas en la bandeja de galletas.

2 Spread the frosting on the crackers with the spoon. Add sprinkles.

2 Pon el glaseado en las galletas con la cuchara. Añade las chispitas.

3 Draw windows and doors with the gel icing. Try making other rectangles that you see in your town.

3 Dibuja puertas y ventanas con el glaseado de jalea. Intenta hacer otros rectángulos que ves en tu ciudad.

Glossary

deck — a full set of playing cards; there are 52 cards in a deck; each card is a rectangle.

exchange — to give one thing and to get something back in return; people can exchange checks for cash at banks.

measure — to find out the size of something; rulers are rectangles that people use to measure or draw straight lines.

note — a written symbol that stands for a musical sound

piano — a large keyboard instrument; pressing down on the black and white keys on a piano makes different sounds.

speed — the rate that something moves; speeds can be slow or fast; speed limit signs are rectangles.

Internet Sites

FactHound offers a safe, fun way to find Internet sites related to this book. All of the sites on FactHound have been researched by our staff.

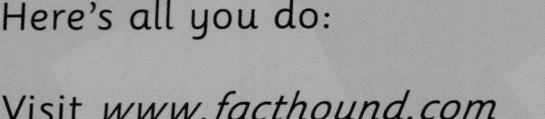

Here's all you do:

Visit *www.facthound.com*

FactHound will fetch the best sites for you!

Glosario

la baraja — juego completo de cartas; una baraja tiene 52 cartas; cada carta es un rectángulo.

cambiar — dar una cosa a cambio de otra; las personas pueden cambiar cheques por dinero en efectivo en los bancos.

medir — encontrar el tamaño de algo; las reglas son rectángulos que las personas usan para medir o dibujar líneas rectas.

la nota — símbolo gráfico que significa un sonido musical

el piano — instrumento grande con teclado; presionar las teclas negras y las blancas en el piano produce diferentes sonidos.

la velocidad — paso al que algo se mueve; la velocidad puede ser lenta o rápida; las señales de límites de velocida son rectángulos.

Sitios de Internet

FactHound brinda una forma segura y divertida de encontrar sitios de Internet relacionados con este libro. Todos los sitios en FactHound han sido investigados por nuestro personal.

Esto es todo lo que tú necesitas hacer:

Visita *www.facthound.com*

¡FactHound buscará los mejores sitios para ti!

Index

Índice